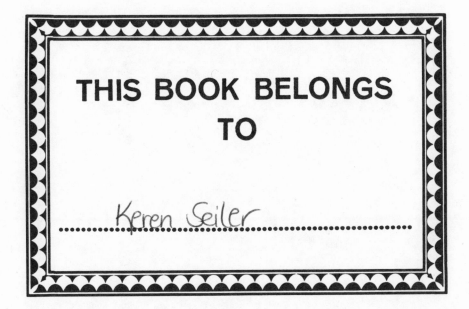

THIS BOOK BELONGS TO

Keren Seiler

This Is Me And My Two Families

An Awareness Scrapbook/Journal for
Children Living in Stepfamilies

by Marla D. Evans

designed by Rick Schuster

Magination Press
An Imprint of Brunner/Mazel, Inc.
New York

ISBN: 0-945354-06-1

Published by Magination Press, an Imprint of Brunner/Mazel, Inc., 19 Union Square West, New York,

MANUFACTURED IN THE UNITED STATES OF AMERICA

10 9 8 7 6 5 4 3

Introduction

Being a parent is an incredibly difficult task for which little preparation and direction has been offered. Being a parent in situations where both mother and father are present in the home is certainly not easy, but being a parent in other situations where divorces, deaths, re-marriages and friendships have changed the child's relationships significantly presents even more perplexity. The parent and the child's ability to cope with the combinations of relationships, expectations and values is crucial to their adaptation to our current lifestyles. Opportunities to share, to explore, to develop and to create issues relevant to both parties are made available to parents and children in *This is Me and My Two Families*. The collaboration necessary for participating in the evolvement of this book with a child is a very strong feature. It would be very difficult to pursue this book with a child and not learn a lot about the child's world. The concepts have intrinsic appeal to most children and the opportunity to draw, to paste their pictures and to dictate their information is enjoyable, as well as developmentally meaningful. The structure used and the topics covered by Evans should be very beneficial to all parents who are dealing with the complexities that step-families present. The format permits self-expression and neither restricts values nor advocates a hypothetical "correct" response. I endorse it as a useful and enjoyable experience for parents dealing with these issues.

John A. Gorman, Ph.D.
Clinical Psychologist
Chapel Hill, NC

Dedication
To Nick Menache and Brenda Brough

Acknowledgements
For their support, I wish to thank my family,
Nancy Pulver for her great literary skills,
my friends, and all those kind enough
to give me advice when I asked.

About the Author
M.D. Evans was a step-parent for four years. She has a post graduate
degree in education from the University of California at Berkeley.

About the Designer
Rick Schuster, a freelance designer, experienced a step-parent
relationship for many years. Through this he became very supportive in
the design and production of this book.

Dear **This Is Me and My Two Families** owners:

This book is for children living in two families. It was created for children and adults to work on together, to improve understanding through talking, writing and art.

Living in two families, for whatever reason, can be extremely challenging for anyone. Oftentimes children in this situation find life very confusing. They find it hard to express their emotions, and are often left feeling helpless and afraid.

In order for children to be healthy and happy, they must learn to communicate their needs by expressing themselves in a noncritical atmosphere. When a child in a household is unhappy, family harmony is disrupted. Therefore, we must encourage our children to talk to us about how they are feeling in order to help strengthen our families.

One of the most positive aspects of this self-discovery book is that it gives both adult and child the opportunity to work together on sensitive subjects in a non-threatening, supportive manner over a comfortable period of time. It allows unspoken subjects to surface so that they may be openly discussed. This will lead to a greater understanding of the child's needs and how they can be met.

This Is Me and My Two Families can be used as a valuable process tool or as an introduction and aid to a counselor or psychologist.

We *can* succeed at opening our lines of communication. I hope that this book helps you in that pursuit.

Most sincerely,

M. D. Evans
Author

A Few Words About Children and Adults Working Together to Use This Book

• This awareness scrapbook/journal is designed for children who live in two stepfamilies to work on with an adult or adults in each family. It has two identical chapters, one for each family as a separate unit.

• Exploring this book together can be a rewarding experience for all parties and can lead to important communication between the child and the adults.

• There are, however, some sections that the child or the helping adult may find emotionally difficult to respond to, so it is possible that:

  • The participants may want to skip over some sections. Maybe they will return to work on them at a later time.

  • Some adults may not want to work with the child on the book. Maybe they will change their minds at a later time.

• If there is no adult living in one of the two family units who is willing to help the child with the book, perhaps an older sibling or stepsibling, a grandparent or stepgrandparent, an uncle or aunt will participate. Or, the child might ask for assistance from other grown-ups he or she trusts, such as a teacher, a neighbor, a friend, a counselor, a therapist, etc. If necessary, the child can work on the book independently.

- Each category of this book has a large area available for a drawing, painting, or photograph which reflects the child's visual perspectives.

- Each category consists of sentences with blank spaces for the child's facts, feelings and opinions.

- Where necessary, instructions in parentheses are added beneath the blanks, to more specifically guide the child.

- In sections requesting information about family members, special consideration has been attempted to include all biological and non-biological members.

- When the words "male adult" or "female adult" are used, the child's special names for these people can be used.

- A suggestion is to cut out introductory pages after you have read them and those pages that are not applicable to your child.

- Regular felt tip pens, glue, crayons, etc. are fine to use, however permanent ink markers will soak through the paper.

- There are no right or wrong answers.

- **Take your time working on your book and have a great time doing it!**

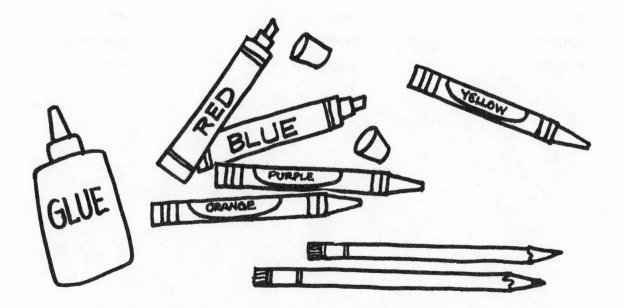

Descriptive Words Guide

You may use these words or find new descriptive words to help with your book.

alone	funny	polite
amazed	fussy	protective
angry	furious	puzzled
anxious	good	sad
awful	great	selfish
bad	guilty	sick
beautiful	happy	silly
bored	helpful	smart
busy	horrible	special
cheerful	important	strange
confused	jealous	strong
curious	joyful	surprised
depressed	kind	terrible
dizzy	lazy	tired
drowsy	marvelous	useful
excited	mean	weird
fair	nice	wild
fantastic	perfect	wonderful
friendly	pleasant	worried

Table of Contents

This Is Me

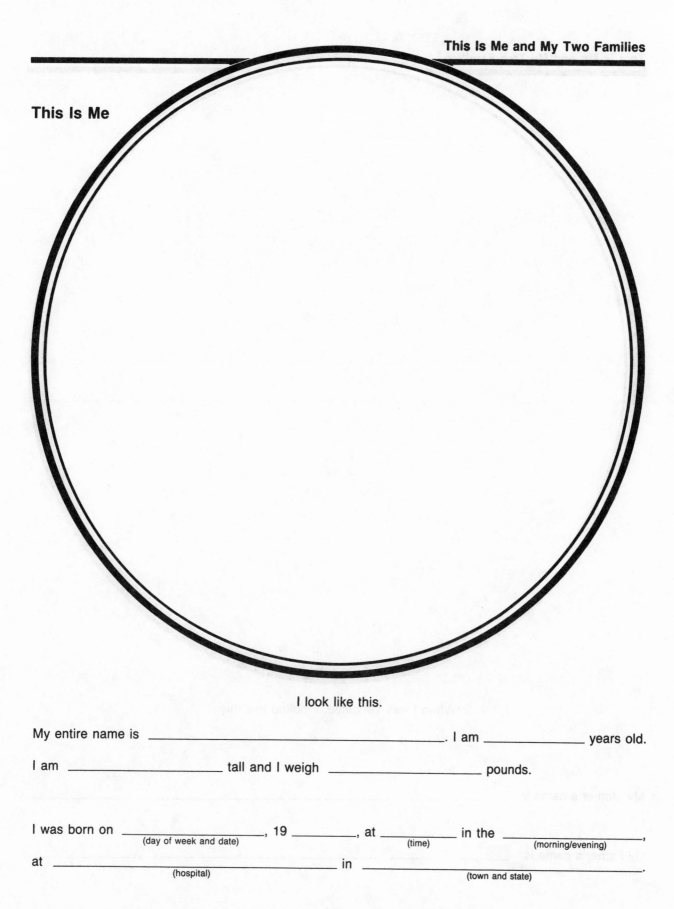

I look like this.

My entire name is _____. I am _____ years old.

I am _____ tall and I weigh _____ pounds.

I was born on _____, 19 _____, at _____ in the _____,
                 (day of week and date)   (time)   (morning/evening)

at _____ in _____.
               (hospital)   (town and state)

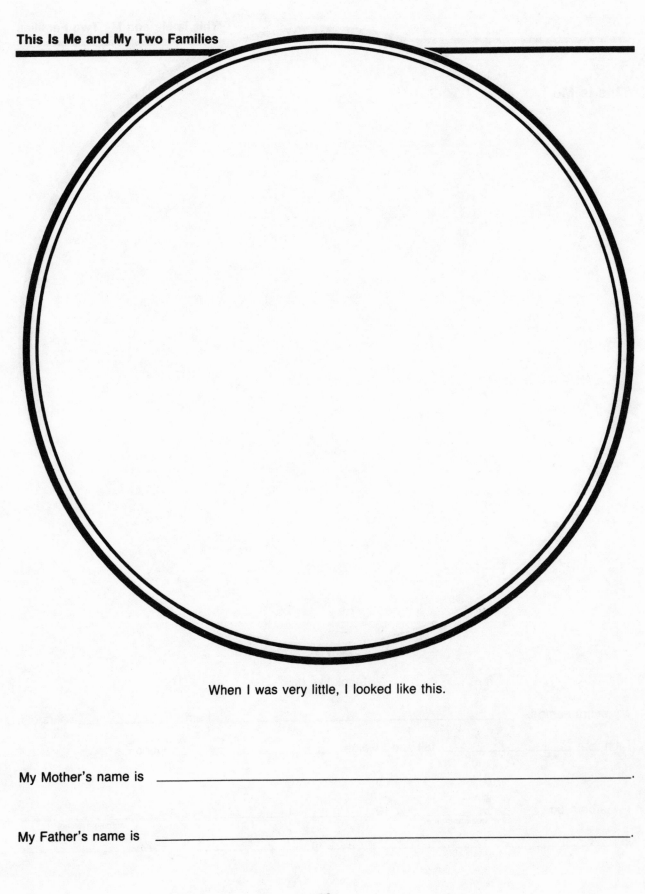

When I was very little, I looked like this.

My Mother's name is _____.

My Father's name is _____.

Myself

This is what I look like when I'm happy.

This is what I look like when I'm sad.

This is what I look like when I _____.

I like myself because _____.

Sometimes I don't like myself because _____.

This Is Me and My Two Families

I'm happiest when _____.

I'm saddest when _____.

I get jealous when _____.

I'm funniest when _____.

I laugh the most when _____.

I make other people laugh the most when _____.

If I had a magic potion, I'd _____.

The thing that makes me the most angry is _____.

When I'm angry I _____.

When others are angry I _____.

When I'm happy I _____.

If I could change something about myself, I'd change _____.

My worst habit is _____.

The thing I like to talk about the most is _____.

The thing I don't like to talk about is _____.

If I could be <u>anybody</u> in the whole wide world, I'd be _____

because _____.

If I could be <u>anything</u> in the whole wide world I'd be _____

because _____.

One of
My Families

My home looks like this.

One Of My Homes

The address of one of my homes is _____.

I started living in this home _____ ago.
(months, years)

The thing I like best about my home is _____.

The thing I like least about my home is _____.

Maybe I could help this bad thing get better by _____.

The chores I'm supposed to do around my home are _____.

The chores I like doing are _____.

The chores I don't like doing are _____.

When I don't do what I'm supposed to do, _____.
(what happens)

The toys I keep in this home that I like best are _____.

Mostly, I play with my toys in _____ with _____.
(what room)   (who)

The room that I don't like very much is _____. I don't think I like it very much

because _____.

My very favorite room is _____. I like it so much because _____

_____.

I live in this house _____.
(how much of the time)

17

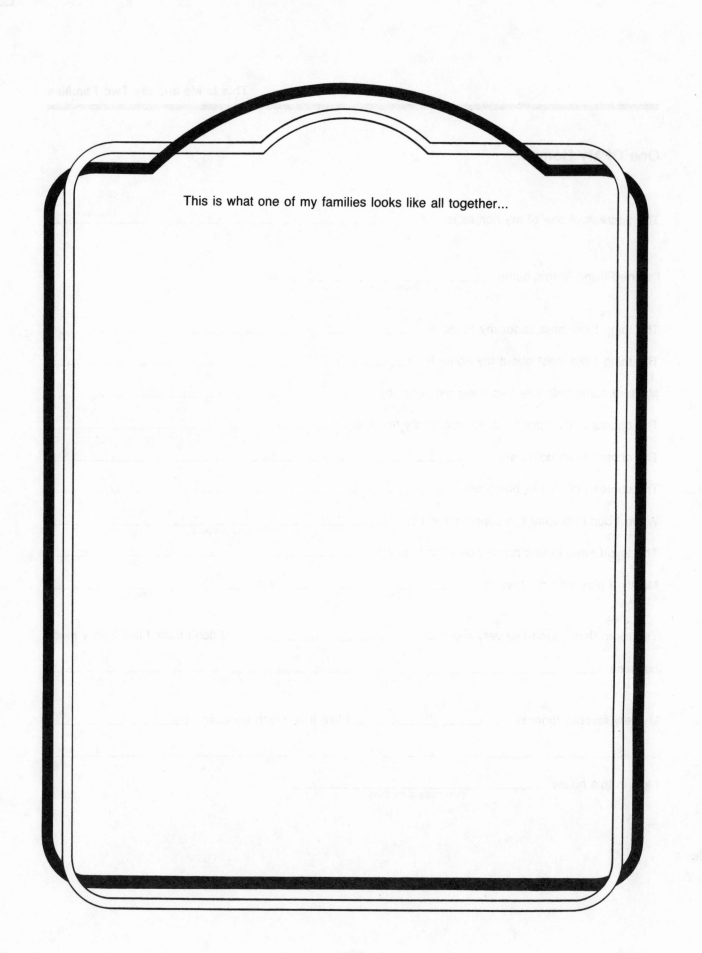

This is what one of my families looks like all together...

My Family

In this home I live with _____.

We do lots of things together like _____.

The best thing I think we've ever done together is _____.

The worst thing I think we've ever done together is _____.

Things we laugh about the most together are _____.

The person in our family who makes us all laugh the most is _____.

_____ makes us laugh usually because _____.
(that person)

But sometimes we have problems, mainly because _____.

When there are problems, there are usually fights. Fighting makes me feel _____

and I usually _____.
(what do you do when fights are going on)

During fights, _____ usually _____.
(mother/stepmother/female adult)   (what does she do?)

During fights, _____ usually _____.
(father/stepfather/male adult)   (what does he do?)

The other kids in my family usually _____during fights.
(what do they do?)

Our fights are usually over when _____.

The best thing about my family is _____.

If I could change any thing about my family, it would be _____.

If I could buy anything for my family, I'd buy _____.

Here I am with my _____...

Parents/Stepparents/Adults In This Family

The thing I like doing the most with the adults in this family is _____.

_____ and I do special things together like _____.
(Father/Stepfather/Male Adult)

Sometimes he thinks I should _____.
(What kinds of things does he think you should do)

When I _____ well, he _____. When I don't do it well,
(something you do)

he _____.

When he's mad at me, he _____.

It makes me feel _____ when he's mad.

One of the best things he and I have ever done is _____.

We talk _____. What we talk mostly about is_____.
(how much)

The thing I like the best about my _____ is _____.
(Father/Stepfather/Male Adult)

_____ and I do special things together like _____.
(Mother/Stepmother/Female Adult)

Sometimes she thinks I should _____.

When I do it well, she _____. When I don't do it well,

she _____. Then I feel _____.
(how do you feel)

She and I have the most trouble when_____.

When she's mad at me, she _____.

One of the best things she and I ever did together was _____.

We talk _____. What we talk about the most is _____.
(how much)

The thing I like the best about my _____ is _____.
(Mother/Stepmother/Female Adult)

Here I am with my _____.
(brothers/stepbros./sisters/stepsis./other)

Brothers/Stepbrothers/Sisters/Stepsisters/Boys, Girls In This Family

I have _____ named _____.
⎯⎯(how many)(brothers/stepbro. or other)⎯⎯⎯⎯⎯⎯⎯⎯(names or nicknames)⎯⎯

I have _____ named _____.
⎯⎯(how many)(sisters/stepsis. or other)⎯⎯⎯⎯⎯⎯⎯⎯(names or nicknames)⎯⎯

We have good times together, especially when we _____.

One of the best things I ever remember doing with _____.
⎯⎯⎯⎯⎯⎯⎯⎯⎯(sibling or stepsibling or other)⎯⎯⎯⎯⎯

is _____.

One thing I didn't like doing with _____ was _____
⎯⎯⎯⎯⎯(sibling/stepsibling/other)⎯⎯⎯⎯

_____. I didn't like it because _____

_____ .

When we kids are all together, sometimes we fight. Mostly what we fight about is _____

_____. The fight is usually over when _____

_____. I get mad at _____ the most
⎯⎯⎯⎯⎯⎯⎯⎯⎯(which sibling)⎯⎯⎯⎯

because _____.

_____ gets mad at me the most because _____.
⎯(which sibling)⎯

I talk to _____ the most. Most of the time we like to talk about _____
⎯⎯⎯(which sibling)⎯⎯

_____. I feel _____ about talking to _____
⎯⎯⎯⎯⎯(how do you feel)⎯⎯⎯⎯⎯⎯⎯(him/her)⎯

because _____.

Having _____ is special because _____.
⎯⎯(brothers/stepbros./sisters/stepsis./other)⎯⎯

Here I am with my _____.
(grandparent/stepgrandparents/grandadults)

24

Grandparents/Stepgrandparents/Grandadults In This Family

I have _____ in this family. I have special names for them like
<small>(how many grandparents/stepgrandparents/grandadults)</small>

_____ .

The most wonderful thing about _____ is _____
<small>(grandparents/stepgrandparents/grandadults)</small>

_____ .

The most difficult thing about _____ is _____
<small>(grandparents/stepgrandparents/grandadults)</small>

_____ .

A fun thing that _____ and I have done is _____.
<small>(which grand/stepgrand)</small>

But the best thing _____ and I have done is _____.
<small>(which grand/stepgrand)</small>

Mostly I talk to _____. What we talk about the most is
<small>(which grand/stepgrand or other)</small>

_____ .

I help my _____ by _____
<small>(grand/stepgrand)</small>

and they help me by _____ .

The best thing I think I ever did for them was _____ .

I liked doing it because _____ .

Here we are eating.

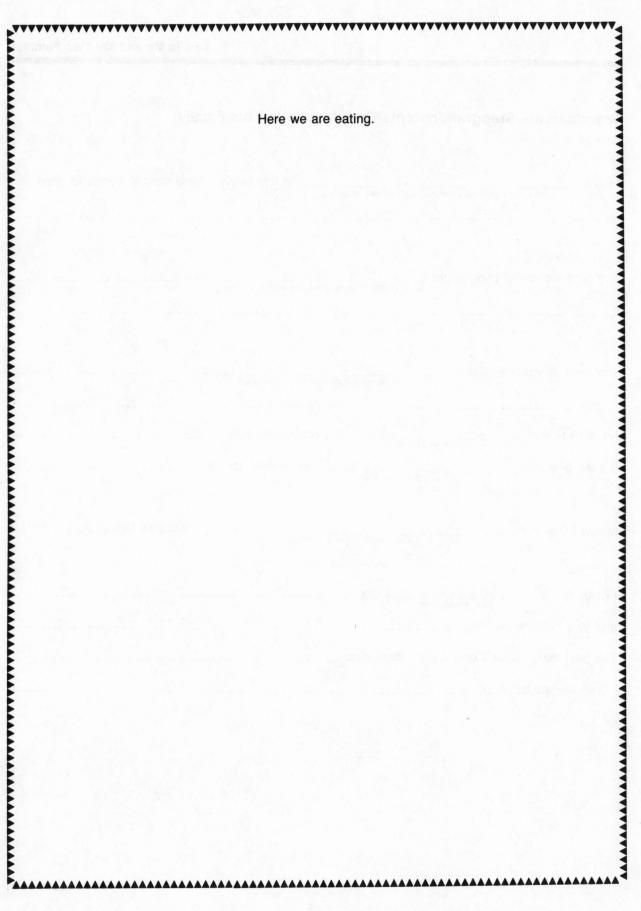

Food

My family and I eat _____ together.
(breakfast, lunch, dinner, snacks)

Our favorite meal is _____.

My favorite meal is _____ because _____.

My least favorite meal is _____ because _____.

I like to eat _____.
(amount)

The meal I seem to have trouble at is _____. I think I have

trouble during it because _____.

The thing I should start doing to have less trouble at that meal is _____.

I have made certain foods, like _____.

_____ taught me how to make _____
(Who)   (what foods)

I feel _____ about making _____ because _____
(how did you feel)   (what kind of food)

_____ .

Once I made _____ for _____ and it was _____.
(what food)   (whom)

The food I just can't stand is _____.

If I don't want to eat it, _____.
(what happens)

Here I am with _____.
(which pet/pets)

Pets

We live with _____ pets.
(how many)

We have a _____ named _____ and a _____ named
(what kind of animal)   (what kind of animal)

_____ .

My favorite pet is _____ . _____ mostly takes care
(who)

of _____ . I feel _____ about taking care of pets because
(pet's name)   (how do you feel)

_____ .

The animal I love most in the whole wide world is _____ because _____

_____ .

The animal I do not like is _____ because _____

_____ .

If I could be any animal in the world, I would be _____

because _____ .

I feel _____ about my family having pets because _____ .
(how do you feel)

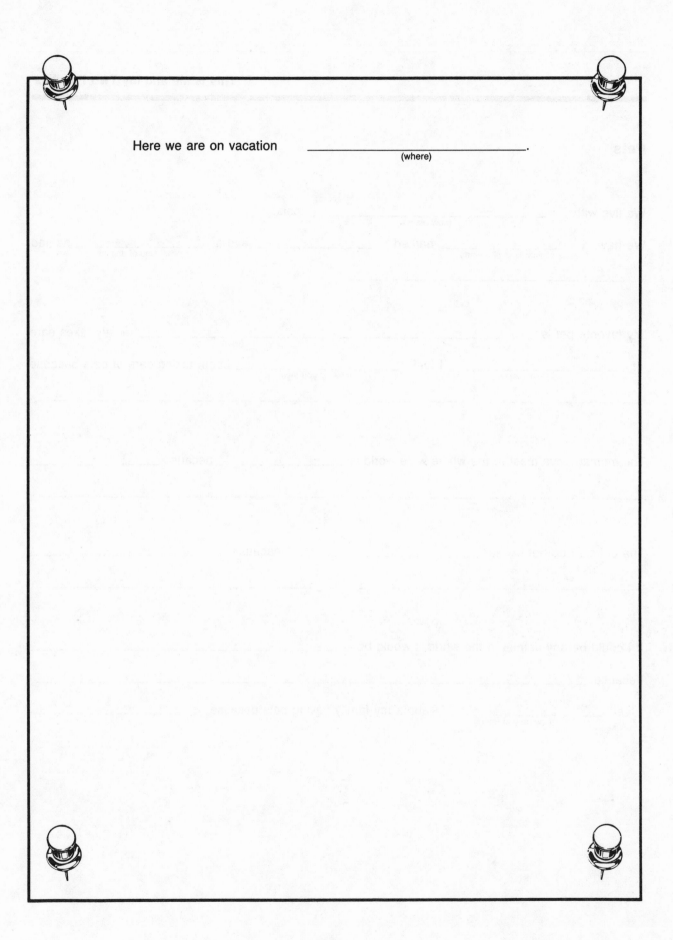

Here we are on vacation _____.
(where)

Vacations

We all go on vacations sometimes. We like to go during _____ the most.
(which season)

The place we usually go to is _____.

The best thing about vacations is _____.

The worst thing about vacations is _____.

I remember once when _____

_____.
(describe an experience you remember very well on a vacation.)

It made me feel _____.

The place I love going the most is _____ because _____

_____.

The place I hate going the most is _____ because _____

_____.

If I could go anywhere in the world, I'd go to _____ with

_____ because _____.
(whom)

One place I would never want to go to is _____ because _____

_____ .

The thing I like to do best on a vacation is _____ because _____

_____.

The worst thing to do on a vacation is _____ because _____

_____.

One of My Families

My home looks like this.

One Of My Homes

The address of one of my homes is _____.

I started living in this home _____ ago.

(months, years)

The thing I like best about my home is _____.

The thing I like least about my home is _____.

Maybe I could help this bad thing get better by _____.

The chores I'm supposed to do around my home are _____.

The chores I like doing are _____.

The chores I don't like doing are _____.

When I don't do what I'm supposed to do, _____.

(what happens)

The toys I keep in this home that I like best are _____.

Mostly, I play with my toys in _____ with _____.

(what room)   (who)

The room that I don't like very much is _____. I don't think I like it very much

because _____.

My very favorite room is _____. I like it so much because _____

_____.

I live in this house _____.

(how much of the time)

35

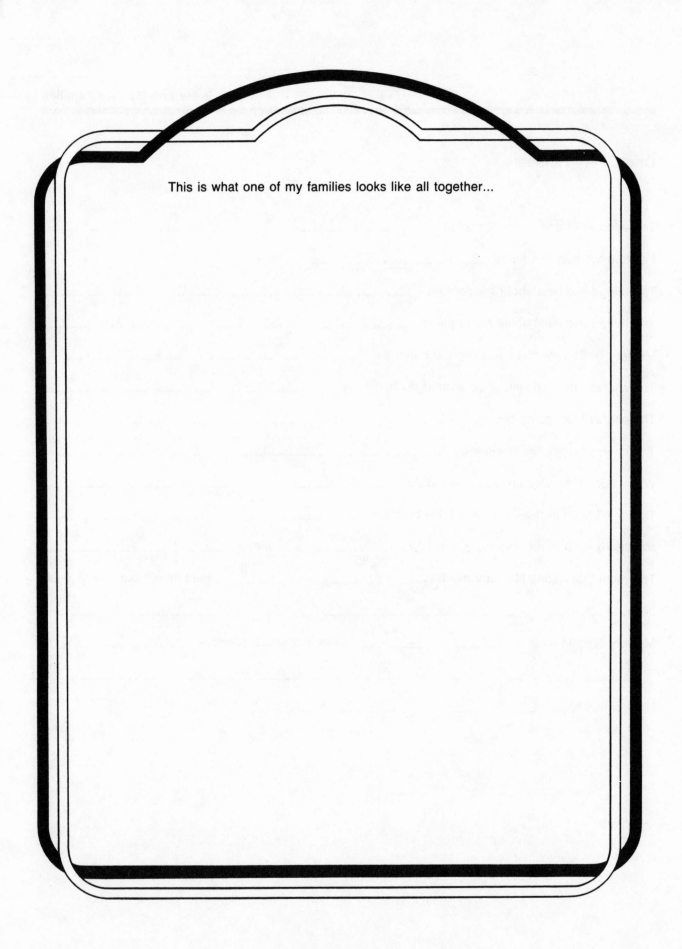

This is what one of my families looks like all together...

My Family

In this home I live with _____.

We do lots of things together like _____.

The best thing I think we've ever done together is _____.

The worst thing I think we've ever done together is _____.

Things we laugh about the most together are _____.

The person in our family who makes us all laugh the most is _____.

_____ makes us laugh usually because _____.
(that person)

But sometimes we have problems, mainly because _____.

When there are problems, there are usually fights. Fighting makes me feel _____

and I usually _____.
(what do you do when fights are going on)

During fights, _____ usually _____.
(mother/stepmother female adult)   (what does she do?)

During fights, _____ usually _____.
(father/stepfather male adult)   (what does he do?)

The other kids in my family usually _____ during fights.
(what do they do?)

Our fights are usually over when _____.

The best thing about my family is _____.

If I could change any thing about my family, it would be _____.

If I could buy anything for my family, I'd buy _____.

Here I am with my _____...

Parents/Stepparents/Adults In This Family

The thing I like doing the most with the adults in this family is _____.

_____ and I do special things together like _____.
(Father/Stepfather/Male Adult)

Sometimes he thinks I should _____.
(What kinds of things does he think you should do)

When I _____ well, he _____. When I don't do it well,
(something you do)

he _____.

When he's mad at me, he _____.

It makes me feel _____ when he's mad.

One of the best things he and I have ever done is _____.

We talk _____. What we talk mostly about is _____.
(how much)

The thing I like the best about my _____ is _____.
(Father/Stepfather/Male Adult)

_____ and I do special things together like _____.
(Mother/Stepmother/Female Adult)

Sometimes she thinks I should _____.

When I do it well, she _____. When I don't do it well,

she _____. Then I feel _____.
(how do you feel)

She and I have the most trouble when _____.

When she's mad at me, she _____.

One of the best things she and I ever did together was _____.

We talk _____. What we talk about the most is _____.
(how much)

The thing I like the best about my _____ is _____.
(Mother/Stepmother/Female Adult)

Here I am with my _____.
(brothers/stepbros./sisters/stepsis./other)

40

Brothers/Stepbrothers/Sisters/Stepsisters/Boys, Girls In This Family

I have _____ named _____.
(how many)(brothers/stepbro. or other) (names or nicknames)

I have _____ named _____.
(how many)(sisters/stepsis. or other) (names or nicknames)

We have good times together, especially when we _____.

One of the best things I ever remember doing with _____.
(sibling or stepsibling or other)

is _____.

One thing I didn't like doing with _____ was _____
(sibling/stepsibling/other)

_____. I didn't like it because _____

_____.

When we kids are all together, sometimes we fight. Mostly what we fight about is _____

_____. The fight is usually over when _____

_____. I get mad at _____ the most
(which sibling)

because _____.

_____ gets mad at me the most because _____
(which sibling)

I talk to _____ the most. Most of the time we like to talk about _____
(which sibling)

_____. I feel _____ about talking to _____
(how do you feel) (him/her)

because _____.

Having _____ is special because _____
(brothers/stepbros./sisters/stepsis./other)

41

Here I am with my _____.
(grandparent/stepgrandparents/grandadults)

42

Grandparents/Stepgrandparents/Grandadults In This Family

I have _____ in this family. I have special names for them like
(how many grandparents/stepgrandparents/grandadults)

_____ .

The most wonderful thing about _____ is _____
(grandparents/stepgrandparents/grandadults)

_____ .

The most difficult thing about _____ is _____
(grandparents/stepgrandparents/grandadults)

_____ .

A fun thing that _____ and I have done is _____ .
(which grand/stepgrand)

But the best thing _____ and I have done is _____ .
(which grand/stepgrand)

Mostly I talk to _____ . What we talk about the most is
(which grand/stepgrand or other)

_____ .

I help my _____ by _____
(grand/stepgrand)

and they help me by _____ .

The best thing I think I ever did for them was _____ .

I liked doing it because _____ .

43

Here we are eating.

44

Food

My family and I eat _____ together.
(breakfast, lunch, dinner, snacks)

Our favorite meal is _____.

My favorite meal is _____ because _____.

My least favorite meal is _____ because _____.

I like to eat _____.
(amount)

The meal I seem to have trouble at is _____. I think I have

trouble during it because _____.

The thing I should start doing to have less trouble at that meal is _____.

I have made certain foods, like _____.

_____ taught me how to make _____.
(Who)   (what foods)

I feel _____ about making _____ because _____.
(how did you feel)   (what kind of food)

_____ .

Once I made _____ for _____ and it was _____.
(what food)   (whom)

The food I just can't stand is _____.

If I don't want to eat it, _____.
(what happens)

Here I am with _____.
                    (which pet/pets)

Pets

We live with _____ pets.
(how many)

We have a _____ named _____ and a _____ named
(what kind of animal)   (what kind of animal)

_____ .

My favorite pet is _____ . _____ mostly takes care
(who)

of _____ . I feel _____ about taking care of pets because
(pet's name)   (how do you feel)

_____ .

The animal I love most in the whole wide world is _____ because _____

_____ .

The animal I do not like is _____ because _____

_____ .

If I could be any animal in the world, I would be _____

because _____ .

I feel _____ about my family having pets because _____ .
(how do you feel)

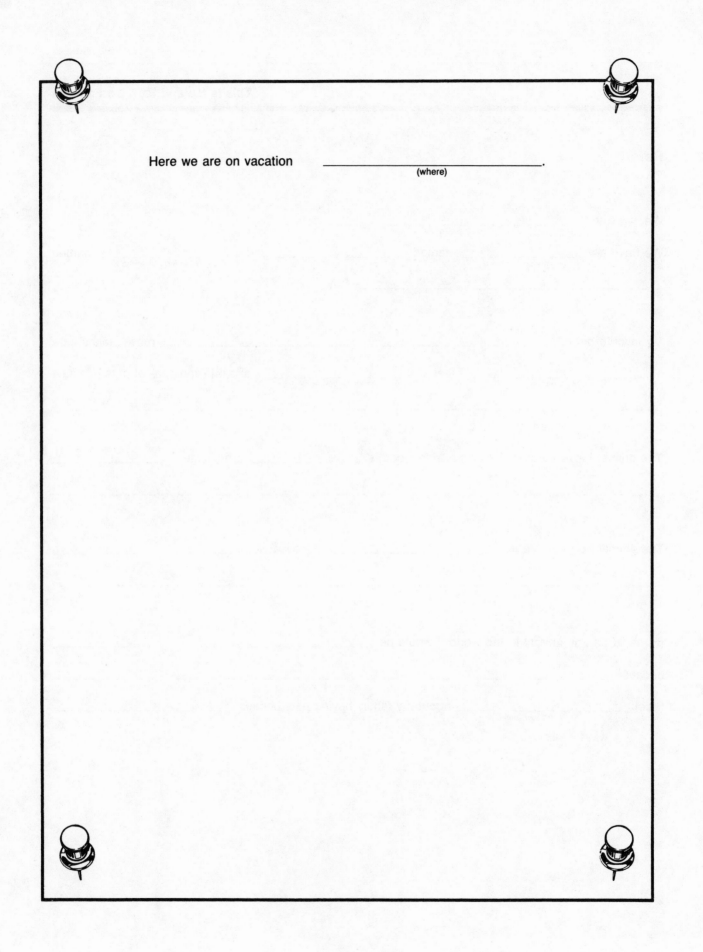

Here we are on vacation _____.
(where)

Vacations

We all go on vacations sometimes. We like to go during _____ the most.
(which season)

The place we usually go to is _____.

The best thing about vacations is _____.

The worst thing about vacations is _____.

I remember once when _____

_____.
(describe an experience you remember very well on a vacation.)

It made me feel _____.

The place I love going the most is _____ because _____

_____.

The place I hate going the most is _____ because _____

_____.

If I could go anywhere in the world, I'd go to _____ with

_____ because _____.
(whom)

One place I would never want to go to is _____ because _____

_____ .

The thing I like to do best on a vacation is _____ because _____

_____.

The worst thing to do on a vacation is _____ because _____

_____.

Other Things About Me

Here I am on my favorite holiday...

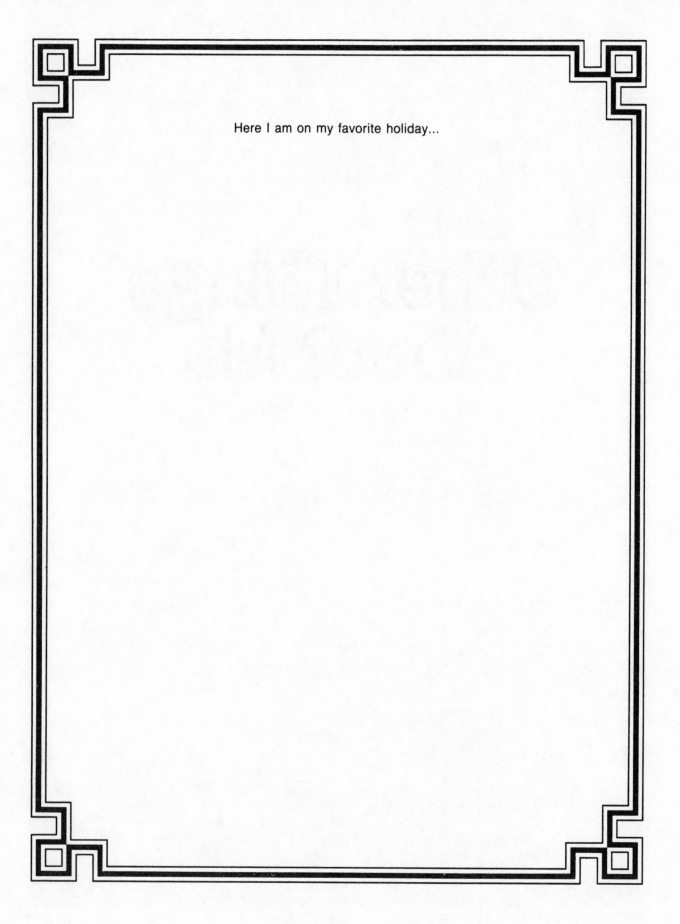

Holidays

My favorite holiday is _____ because _____

_____ .

The holiday I don't like as much is _____ because _____

_____ .

The holiday I remember the most is _____ . I remember it so much because

_____ .

The best thing about holidays is _____ .

The worst thing about holidays is _____ .

I like being with _____ people on holidays because _____
        (how many)

_____ .

If I could invent any holiday I wanted to, it would be called _____

and we would _____ .
        (what special things would you do)

My holiday would be held on _____ and _____
        (what date)   (who)

would be there.

This is my school.

I go to _____ school. I get there in the morning by _____
(which)   (car, truck, walking, how)

and come back from school by _____ when I stay at _____.
(how)   (address)

School

When I stay at _____ , I get to school by _____ and come back home
(other address)   (how)

by _____ .

I'm in the _____ grade.

I feel _____ about school because _____
(how do you feel)

_____ .

I am better in some subjects than others. My better subjects are _____

_____ .

The not-so-good ones are _____ . The not-so-good ones are

tough for me because _____ .

I try _____ to get better at them by _____ .
(how hard do you try)

I guess I'm better at some subjects than others because _____ .

Things we do at school other than work are _____ .

I feel _____ about doing those things because _____ .
(how do you feel)

I _____ homework because _____ . I usually do
(how do you feel)

my homework _____ . I get along with the other kids in my class
(during what part of the day)

_____ because _____
(not so well, pretty well, real well)

_____ .

I know that _____ and _____ live in two families like me.
(name)   (name)

I _____ talked to them about living in too families because _____
(have, have not)

_____ .

The person I talk to the most about school is _____ .

If I could change one thing about school, I'd _____
(what would you change)

_____ .

Here's My Teacher...

My Teacher

My teacher's name is _____.

I _____ my teacher because _____.
(how do you feel)

My teacher is real strict about _____.

My teacher is real nice about _____.

When _____ is real strict, I _____.
(he/she)   (how do you feel)

The best thing my teacher ever did for me is _____.

The best thing I ever did for my teacher is _____.

One thing I did that really made my teacher mad was _____.

I knew my teacher was mad because _____

and I felt _____.

The best teacher I ever had in my life was _____. I liked this teacher

so much because _____.

The worst teacher I ever had in my life was _____ because _____

_____ .

If I were a teacher, one thing I'd do for my students is _____.

One thing I did that really made my teacher happy was _____.

I knew my teacher was happy because _____

and I felt _____.

My teacher _____ I live in two families. I _____ talked to my teacher about
(knows, does not know)   (have, have not)

it because _____.

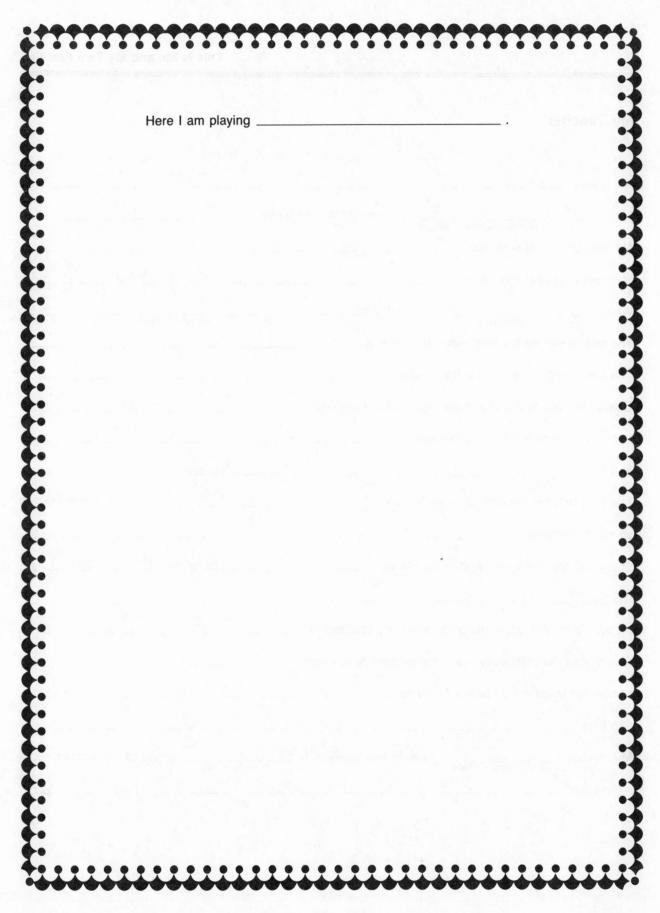

Here I am playing _____ .

Sports/Games

I feel _____ about _____.
(how do you feel)   (which sports or games)

I play _____ _____.
(sport/game)   (a little bit, a medium amount, alot, other)

The best _____ I have ever played is _____.
(sport/game)

I have played it about _____ times and mostly with _____.
(how many)   (whom)

The best thing about playing _____ is _____.
(sports and/or games)

The worst thing about playing _____ is _____.
(sports and/or games)

The person I like playing with the most is _____

because _____.

When I win, I feel _____.

_____.

When I lose, I feel _____.

_____.

At my home on _____ I mostly play _____ with _____.
(address)   (what game)   (whom)

At my home on _____ I mostly play _____ with _____.
(other address)   (what game)   (whom)

Here's me and my best friend...

Here I am with some of my friends...

Friends

The friends that come to my home on _____ the most are _____
(address of one home)

_____ .

Where we play the most at this home is _____ .

The friends that come to my home on _____ the most are _____
(address of other home)

_____ .

Where we play the most at this home is _____ .

I have _____ very good friends. Their names are _____
(how many)

_____ .

I _____ being with more than one friend because _____
(how do you feel)

Sometimes it's hard being with more than one friend because _____

_____ .

The best part of being with friends is _____ .

I think my very best friend is _____ . We've been best friends for

_____ . I knew _____ was my best friend when _____
(how long)   (friend's name)

_____ .

Mostly, we like playing _____ at _____ .
(what)   (where)

The things we talk about most are _____ .

We get in trouble most often when _____ .

When we fight, it's usually about _____ . Our fight's are usually

over when _____ .

One of the best things we ever did together was _____ .

Here I am talking to _____ .

Talking

I spend _____ of time talking.
(a little bit, a medium amount, a lot)

My favorite subjects to talk about are _____.

The things I don't like to talk about are _____.

When I talk the most, I usually do it _____.
(during which part of the day)

At my home on _____, I mostly talk with _____.
(address of one home)

At my home on _____, I mostly talk with _____.
(address of other home)

Talking usually makes me feel _____.
(how)

I think people should talk about how they feel because _____

_____.

I don't think people should talk about how they feel when _____

_____.

Here I am _____ about _____.
(daydreaming/thinking)

Thinking/Daydreaming

What I like to think about the most is _____.

What I like to daydream about the most is _____.

What I don't like thinking about is _____.

The things I think about the most are _____.

The person I think about the most is _____ because

_____.

Some of the places I like to daydream at are _____.

I daydream _____.
(how much)

I think I daydream because _____.

I like to tell _____ what I'm thinking or daydreaming
(who)

about because _____.

The best thought I ever had was _____.

The worst thought I ever had was _____.

The daydream I would like to see come true is _____.

Here's something that scares me...

Scary Things

Certain things scare me. One thing that scares me a lot is _____.

I think it scares me a lot because _____.

I try to stop it from scaring me by _____.

The scariest thing that ever happened to me at my home at _____
(one of your addresses)

was _____. It stopped scaring me when _____

_____.

The scariest thing that ever happened to me at my home at _____
(your other address)

was _____. It stopped scaring me when _____

_____.

Everybody is scared about something. _____ is scared about _____
(which member of family)

_____.

My friend, _____ is scared about _____
(friend)

_____.

I usually talk to _____ about things that scare me.
(whom)

I feel _____ about being scared because _____
(how do you feel)

My favorite scary halloween costume is _____.

My favorite character, _____, in my favorite book,
(character's name)

_____, looks like this...
(title)

Books

I read books _____
(how much)

I read _____ to myself.
(how much)

I read _____ to _____.
(how much)   (whom)

I _____ to read because _____.
(how do you feel)

Sometimes _____ reads to me.
(who)

A character I do not like at all is _____ because
(name of character)

_____.

A character I know that is the most like me is _____ because
_____.

If I could go and live in any book, my choice would be _____
(book title)

because _____.

_____ loves the book _____.
(family member)   (book title)

_____ loves the book _____.
(other family member)   (book title)

I talked to _____ about the last book I read which was _____
(family member)   (book title)

_____.

Mostly, the members of my family _____ to read.
(how do they feel)

Here I am watching T.V.

Television

I feel _____ about television.
(how do you feel)

At my home on _____ , I watch T.V. _____ hours a day.
(address) (how many)

At this home I usually watch _____ with _____.
(which programs) (whom)

At my home on _____ , I watch T.V. _____ hours a day.
(other address) (how many)

At this home I usually watch _____ with _____.
(which programs) (whom)

I think I watch T.V. _____.
(a little bit, a medium amount, a lot)

My favorite show is _____.

I like it so much because _____.

If I could be like anyone or anything on T.V., I would be _____

because _____.

The person or thing on T.V. that I would not want to be is _____

because _____.

The thing I don't like about T.V. is _____ because _____

_____.

The T.V. show I can't stand is _____ because _____

_____.

I like watching T.V. with _____ people.
(how many)

Here I am watching the movie _____ ...

72

Movies

I feel _____ about movies.
(how do you feel)

I go to the movies _____.
(how often)

My favorite movie is _____.

I like it so much because _____.

I went to see it with _____.

The worst movie I ever saw was _____.

It was so bad because _____.

If I could be in any movie I wanted to, I would be _____ in _____
(which character)   (which movie)

because _____.

If I could make a movie, I'd make one about _____.

The movie my family at _____ likes the most is _____.
(address)

The movie my family at _____ likes the most is _____.
(other address)

Here I am sick.

Being Sick

I feel _____ about being sick.
(how do you feel)

I get sick _____.
(not very often, a medium amount, alot)

The things I like to do when I'm sick are _____.

The thing I ask for the most when I'm sick is _____.

The person that gets sick the most in my family at _____ is _____.
(address)

The person that gets sick the most in my family at _____ is _____.
(other address)

The best part about being sick is _____.

The worst part about being sick is _____.

When others are sick in my family, I help to take care of them by _____.

When I am sick, I like being _____ the most.
(with whom)

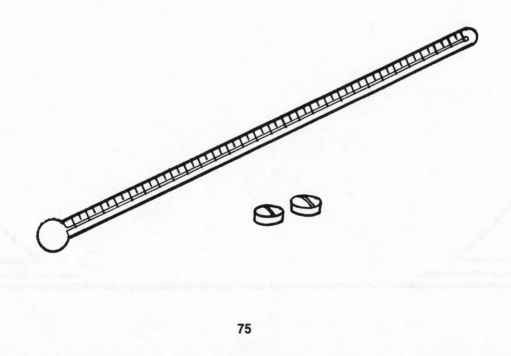

75

Here I am doing my favorite thing.

Things To Do

My favorite thing to do is _____.

I do it _____.
     (how often)

I've been doing it for _____.
              (how long)

If I need help doing it, I usually ask _____.

I guess the reason I like it so much is because _____.

My least favorite thing to do is _____. I just can't

stand it because _____.

I find _____ things to do.
    (lots of, enough, not very many, never any)

Mostly, I like doing things _____.
                (by myself, with 1 other person, with more than 1 person)

Things I would like to do someday _____.

The thing I'd like to do but am afraid to try is _____.

I'm afraid to try it because _____.

Some things that my family at _____ likes to do together are _____.
                (address)

One thing we don't like to do together is _____.

Some things that my family at _____ likes to do together are _____.
                (other address)

One thing we don't like to do together is _____.

If I could do anything in the world I wanted to do, I would _____

_____.

If I could make somebody else do anything in the world, I would _____

_____.

Here I am dreaming.

Dreaming When I Sleep

I remember _____ of my dreams.
(alot, many, or not too many)

My dreams are mostly _____ dreams.
(use a descriptive word)

The best dream I remember having is _____.

The worst dream I remember having is _____.

I talk to _____ about my dreams.
(whom)

I _____ wake up in the middle of the night because of a dream.
(sometimes, never, often)

The way I get back to sleep is _____.

Everybody has bad dreams once in awhile. One bad dream that _____ told me
(family member)

about was _____.

A good dream _____
(family member)

told me about was _____

_____ .

If I could pick any dream to live in, I would pick the one about _____

_____ .

Dreams are _____.

Here something special is happening.

Happenings

Something very special happened to me once. _____

_____ .

I felt _____.

Something awful happened to me once. _____

_____ .

I felt _____.

I felt better when _____.

Something happened to _____ that was _____.
                                (family member)   (descriptive word)

When I found out about it I _____.

I felt _____ about it happening because _____
           (how did you feel)

_____ .

The best thing that could ever happen to me would be _____

_____ .

The worst thing that could ever happen to me would be _____

_____ .

The greatest thing that could happen to anyone would be _____

_____ .

Here I am _____
(doing which talent)

Talents

I have special talents in some things like _____.

I don't think I have any talents in _____.

_____ thinks I'm very talented in _____.

(family member)

I _____ because _____.
   (agree, disagree)

I feel _____ about things I can do well because _____
       (how do you feel)

_____.

I feel _____ about talking about what I'm bad at because _____
       (how do you feel)

_____.

I wish I were more talented in _____.

I think I can get better at some things by _____.
                                            (doing what)

I feel _____ when I see people doing things very well.
       (how do you feel)

Sometimes I wish I were as talented as _____. I would like to do

what _____ they can do because _____.
      (person's name)

My best friend is especially talented in _____.

_____ is very talented in _____.
      (Family member)

I am the most talented in _____.

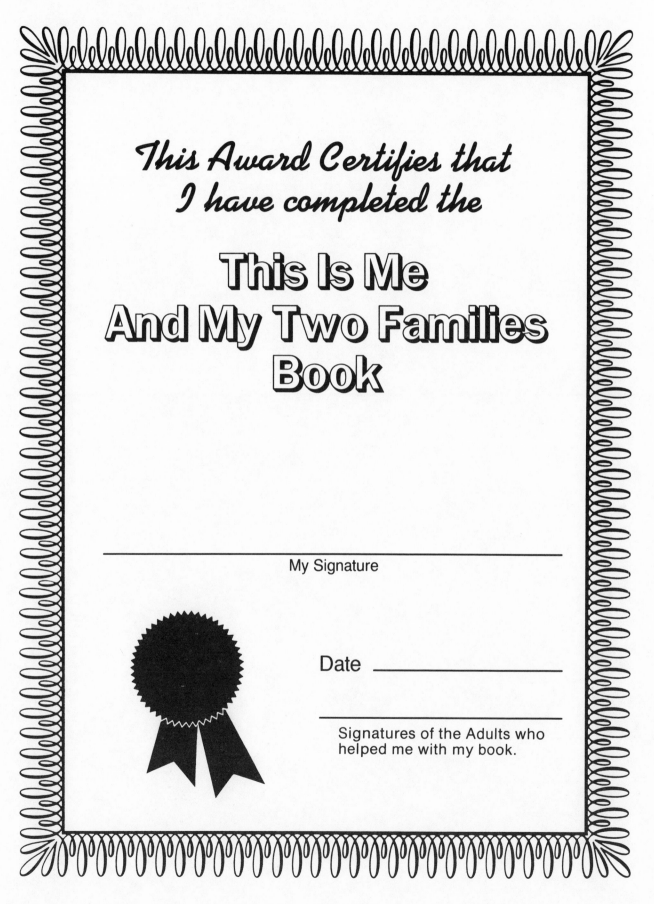

This Award Certifies that I have completed the

This Is Me And My Two Families Book

_____

My Signature

Date _____

_____

Signatures of the Adults who
helped me with my book.